Wealth Creation:
The Solution to Poverty

William R. Luckey

ACTONINSTITUTE
Christian Social Thought Series
Number 24 • Edited by Kevin Schmiesing

Christian Social Thought Series, Number 24

© 2017 by Acton Institute

Acton Institute
for the Study of Religion and Liberty
All rights reserved.

Cover image: Hong Kong Street Market
Source: www.istock.com.

ISBN: 978-1-938948-48-0

ActonInstitute

98 E. Fulton
Grand Rapids, Michigan 49503
Phone: 616.454.3080
Fax: 616.454.9454
www.acton.org

Printed in the United States of America

Contents

Foreword		*v*
I	The Biblical Perspective on Wealth	1
II	The Fathers of the Church on Wealth	7
III	Wealth and Poverty in the Medieval World	11
IV	The Beginning of Wealth Creation	19
V	The Contemporary View of the Church: The Special Case of *Populorum Progressio*	25
VI	The Science of the Creation and Distribution of Wealth	39
References		53
About the Author		59

Foreword

Care for the poor has been a hallmark of Christianity since its beginning in the first century AD. From the Church Fathers to the modern papal encyclical tradition, the call to serve and uplift the poor and marginalized has been consistent and clarion.

Professor William Luckey fully recognizes this call. Yet, he observes, the human innovation reflected in the rapid, widespread increase in wealth from the Industrial Revolution forward provides a new context for the Christian engagement with poverty. The Catholic social tradition, he believes, would benefit from appraising the sources and benefits of wealth creation and considering the lessons therein for how we act individually and in the realm of public policy.

Luckey traces the history Church reflection on poverty and wealth, as well as the history of wealth creation, with a view to promoting this engagement. It is, of course, a long and complicated story—to which justice can hardly be done in such a brief book—but Luckey's admirably succinct treatment captures the essential elements. The creation of wealth requires technical expertise and innovation, to be sure, but it also requires social and cultural support. Something as seemingly mundane as saving, he points out, "implies a kind of morality" as "to consume less than one earns requires self-restraint." And saving is a prerequisite for the accumulation of capital, which is necessary in turn for the further building of wealth.

This increase in wealth may well result in the creation of massive fortunes among the rich, but the more important result to the Christian perspective is that it will provide the means to improve the material welfare of those who are the most vulnerable. In this way, wealth creation is a necessary component of poverty relief.

It is by fostering the attitudes and institutions that provide the context for wealth creation that the Church can make a special contribution to care for the poor, beyond the direct relief that has so distinguished the Church's charitable activity and for which it has been rightly praised. Luckey here offers an informed reflection on how Catholics and other Christians might more effectively promote this wealth-creative culture, one that will in turn more effectively lift our brothers and sisters in need out of poverty and desperation. "If Catholics are serious about improving the lives of the poor," the author insists, "we must be serious about understanding the sources of wealth creation." May our encounter with this reflection assist us in living out the exalted yet challenging command to love our neighbors as ourselves.

Kevin Schmiesing
Acton Institute

1 The Biblical Perspective on Wealth

Christians are generally aware that they have an obligation to assist the poor. It is preached from pulpits, written in books, taught in schools. Some go so far as to make aid to the poor the sole aim of Christianity—the proponents of the "social gospel." This is particularly prevalent in Catholic universities, with which I have some familiarity. Frequently in such universities' statements attempting to prove that they are Catholic there is no pledge of strict adherence to the Magisterium of the Church but instead a commitment to help the poor.

Such statements seem uncontroversial—after all, who does not want to help the poor? The issue becomes more contentious, however, when discussion turns to the best method for doing so. Without question, Scripture and Sacred Tradition lay an obligation on believers to assist those in need. At the same time, these sources do not lend much support to the idea that the state is the remedy for the problems of the poor. What, then, is the biblical perspective on wealth and poverty?

While some passages of the Old Testament suggest that wealth indicates the favor of God, the dominant message is that human beings are stewards of their wealth, which is a gift from God, and that wealth and goodness are not necessarily companions. In Deuteronomy 8:17–18, God warns the Israelites not to attribute their ability to procure wealth to their own abilities but to God who gave the ability. Job speaks about how the wealthy live longer and prosper, but they are not necessarily good. Wealth is not a sign of goodness. Job even says (Job 21–25) that it would have been sinful for him to rejoice in his wealth. Psalm 49:6 points out that man's wealth can never save him, and 49:10 reminds us that all die and leave their wealth to others.

Proverbs (10:16) tells us that the wage of the righteous leads to life, but the gain of the wicked leads to sin. The same book (19:4 and 19:7) demonstrates the plight of the poor, showing that riches cause us to be surrounded by sycophants, but all the poor man's friends leave him, and his brother hates him. Therefore, one should not depend on dishonest wealth because it will not help one in the day of calamity (Sir. 5:8). Ecclesiastes 6 speaks of the fact that the wealthy man is frustrated in his desires because his problem tends to be his insatiable desires that can never be satisfied with material things.[1]

In many places in the Old Testament our duties to the poor are stressed. Exodus 22:25 says that if one lends money to a poor person, one does not become a creditor and may not charge interest. Essentially, this type of loan is a gift, not a business transaction. If the person prospers and is able to pay it back, so much the better, but, especially in an agricultural society where people can become poor overnight by the whims of nature, this loan becomes an emergency.

The New Testament continues this line of reasoning but builds on it, placing the new law of love and sacrifice above it. Many of the examples that Jesus gives in the Gospels reflect the economic situation in the Palestine of his time. Generally speaking, people got wealthy by exploiting others rather than by creating wealth. This was usually done through (1) high land rents that gave a huge income to the landowners or (2) regular

---

[1] This insatiability is the reason that demand for goods tends to outstrip supply—what economists call *scarcity*.

taxation that created a sumptuous-living political class. The first situation is illustrated in the parable of the man whose harvest is so great that he has to build new barns to contain it (Luke 12:16–21). The man felt very secure because he had a huge amount of grain. "But God said to him, 'Fool! This night your soul is required of you; and the things you have prepared, whose will they be?'" Another example of an owner who extracts huge rents is found in the parable of Lazarus and the rich man (Luke 16:19–31). The rich man has enormous wealth, while Lazarus has nothing and sits outside the rich man's door with sores all over his body, begging for his mere subsistence. When their lives are over, Lazarus goes to the bosom of Abraham, but the rich man goes to hell.

An example of the second kind is given in the story of the rich young man who comes to Jesus asking what he can do to be saved (Luke 18:18–27). The original Greek uses the word αρχων for the rich man, meaning "ruler." He could have been a ruler of the synagogue or a state functionary. The implication is that his wealth was acquired by way of taxation or the charging of temple fees. Jesus tells him that if he keeps the commandments he can be saved, but also that he lacks something. He asks him to sell all he has and give the proceeds to the poor and then become a follower of Jesus. The young ruler becomes depressed, "for he was very rich." Jesus remarks on how it is almost impossible for a rich man to enter the kingdom of heaven. In response to the question, "Then who can be saved?" Jesus responds, "What is impossible with men is possible with God."

The economic background of the time helps to explain Christ's statements about wealth. Landlords took the crops, or charged enormous fees as rents. Governments used taxes mostly for the ruler's income and those of his flunkies. Both rulers and owners provided just enough services so that the wealth kept coming in. Meanwhile the people lived a hand-to-mouth existence, more or less.[2] Therefore, the normative means of achieving great wealth was not to create it by contributing to economic innovation and efficiency but to redistribute existing wealth from poor to rich. Thus the seemingly harsh tones of the Old Testament and of Jesus and even the fathers of the church about wealth are explicable. It was rare for a person to become rich without depriving others of the chance to lead a decent life. This is why, in the Christian dispensation, it is by virtue that one is judged, not by wealth, status, class, or position.

This also sheds light on the Magnificat, the prayer of Mary during her visitation to Elizabeth. In that spontaneous outpouring of the Spirit, Mary says that God "has scattered the proud in the imagination [διανοια (thoughts, understanding)] of their hearts" (Luke 1:51). "He has put down the mighty from their thrones, and exalted those of low degree" (Luke 1:52). Finally, "he has filled the hungry with good things, and the rich he has sent empty away" (Luke 1:53). Is this a call for political revolution as the liberation theologians would have it? To think so would rob this section of Scripture of its spiritual essence, and defy all that the Old Testament said about rich and poor. William Barclay explains the passage in its properly spiritual sense:

> (i) *He scatters the proud in the plans of their hearts.* That is a moral revolution. Christianity is the death of pride. Why? Because if a man sets his life beside that of Christ it tears the last vestiges of pride from him.... (ii) He casts down the mighty—he exalts the humble. That is a social revolution. Christianity puts an end to the world's labels and prestige.... When we have realized what Christ

---

[2] See the discussion in Igino Giordani, *The Social Message of Jesus* (Boston: St. Paul Editions, 1977), chap. 10. Also, Henri Daniel-Rops, *Daily Life in the Time of Jesus*, trans. Patrick O'Brian (New York: Hawthorn Books, 1962), pt. 2, chap. 3.

has done for all men, it is no longer possible to speak about a common man. (iii) He has filled those who are hungry ... those who are rich he has sent empty away. That is an economic revolution. A non-Christian society is an acquisitive society where each man is out to amass as much as he can get. A Christian society is a society where no man dares to have too much while others have too little, where every man must get only to give away.[3]

Notice that Barclay's comment puts the onus of charity on every man. The essence of the passage cited in the Magnificat is that those having much wealth, regardless of their public status, are not as important as the poor, humble man—unless they use their wealth to help the less fortunate.

---

[3] William Barclay, *The Gospel of Luke*, rev. ed. (Philadelphia: Westminster Press, 1975), 15–16.

II The Fathers of the Church on Wealth

The church fathers affirm the scriptural message that it is not wealth or poverty that is the criterion of goodness. St. John Chrystostom's *On Wealth and Poverty* typifies the fathers' ideas on the subject and continues the scriptural themes. He says that life is like a stage play:

> As long as the audience remains in their seats, the masks are valid; but when evening overtakes them, and the play is ended, and everyone goes out, the masks are cast aside. He who is king inside the theatre is found to be a coppersmith outside. The masks are removed, the deceit departs, the truth is revealed.... So it is also in life and its end. The present world is a theater, the conditions of men are roles: wealth and poverty, ruler and ruled, and so forth. When this day is cast aside, and that terrible night comes ... when each person is judged with his works—not each person with his wealth, not each person with his office, not each person with his authority, not each person with his power, but each person with his works, whether he is ruler or king, a woman or a man, when He requires an account of our life and our good deeds, not

> the weight of our reputation, not the slightness of our poverty, not the tyranny of our disdain.[1]

The fact that this needed to be said, even though the Roman Empire had long been officially Christian, demonstrates that Christianity had not yet been fully acculturated by the population of the empire. Eric Voegelin points out that the empire might have been officially Christian but in general its population was not. They still retained their pagan ideas, worldviews, and many practices. Even sincere Christians sometimes tried to unite pagan and Christian notions, as when it was proposed that there should be three emperors who would mirror the Blessed Trinity.[2] In other words, the early Christians lived in a pagan society even after official Christianization, and therefore they faced many of the same problems as the Hebrews and the residents of the Holy Land at the time of Jesus.

This means that neither Jesus nor the early church focused on remedying poverty in general but instead focused on helping the poor. As both the Old Testament and Jesus himself said, the poor will always be with us. The obligation of the well-off is to help the poor by giving of their substance as motivated by love. In this sense, the poor are given by God for the rest of us. The Christian owner of an enterprise is required to treat his workers justly and with love. Those who have wealth are not allowed to hoard it. In fact, "one of the human factors responsible for the more rapid success of Christianity in comparison with the other religions supported by the state or spread by the army, was precisely this interest that the Church brought to the

---

[1] St. John Chrysostom, *On Wealth and Poverty*, trans. Catharine P. Roth (Crestwood, NY: St. Vladimir's Seminary Press, 1984), 109.

[2] Eric Voegelin, "The Struggle for Representation in the Roman Empire," pt. 3, in *The New Science of Politics* (Chicago: University of Chicago Press, 1952), 76–106.

solution of the human problems of property, money, and labor, a solution conditioned by the precepts of charity and justice."[3]

Although some Christian writers expressed negative opinions concerning business and commerce, there were more positive assessments as well. The influential church father Tertullian wrote:

> But there is another sheet of wrong-doing upon the sheet against us [Christians]. We are said to be unprofitable in business. How so—when we are human beings and live along side of you—men with the same ways, the same dress and furniture, the same necessities, if we are to live? For we are not Brahmans, naked sages of India, forest-dwellers, exiles from life. We remember that we owe gratitude to God, the Lord, the Creator. We reject no fruit of His labours. We are of course temperate—not to use His gifts to excess or amiss. So, not without your forum, not without your meat-market, not without your baths, shops, factories, your inns and market—days, and the rest of the life of buying and selling, we live with you—in this world. We sail ships, we as well as you, and along with you; we go to the wars, to the country, to market with you. Our arts and yours work together; our labor is openly at your service. How can we seem unprofitable to your business, when we live with you, and our living depends on you, I do not know.[4]

Tertullian's observations indicate that early Christians were engaged in business alongside their pagan countrymen, and that there was no particular stigma attached to this participation in commerce.

---

[3] Igino Giordani, *The Social Message of the Church Fathers* (Boston: St. Paul Editions, 1977), 254.

[4] Tertullian, *Apology* XLII, 1–3.

In summary, the message of the early church concerning wealth includes the following points:

- Wealth and poverty are seen as given by God.
- Wealth at the time was almost always acquired by taking it.
- The wealthy must not hoard their wealth but freely give it to the poor.
- The poor are not automatically blessed with goodness because of their poverty, nor are the rich blessed with goodness because of their wealth or power.
- The rich are commanded to be detached from their wealth; the poor are reminded not to be avaricious.

These points must be understood within the context of the time. The mentality of the whole era was static. Non-Christian and Christian alike failed to understand that wealth could be dynamic, that people innovate, situations change, and people adapt to those circumstances. Similarly, there was no theory of wealth creation; that is, no one ever said that it is good to start businesses, supplying the needs of others, and in turn employing people who would not otherwise be employed, saving up the wealth to increase the enterprise, hiring more people, and supplying new and better things—those benefits of business that are evident in a dynamic economy.[5]

---

[5] See Robert G. Kennedy, "Does a Business Corporation Have a Responsibility to Society?" *Religion and Liberty* 13, no. 6, accessed February 12, 2011, http://www.acton. org/pub/religion-liberty/volume-13-number-6/does-business-corporation-have-responsibility-soci.

III Wealth and Poverty in the Medieval World

Rome was typical of a society that operates on a caste system. In a caste system, there is general immobility among classes. If one was born an *equites* (the lower of the aristocratic classes), one could not become a member of the patrician or senatorial class without some kind of special benefit conferred by a ruler, usually involving a large estate. Freed men were not considered citizens but could engage in commercial activity, some very successfully. Slaves, of course, belonged completely to their owners who could do with them as they pleased. The problem of the caste system is that if one is prohibited from moving to a higher class by his own efforts, one has no incentive to try.

The early medieval period of history was an excellent example of a caste system but certainly not the only one. By the year 395 AD the days of the Roman Empire were clearly numbered by the barbarian invasions. By the 500s the Western Roman Empire was in the hands of the Germanic tribes. Some of Rome's government traditions remained under Germanic rule, and mostly that rule was seen as a personal attribute of the ruler, rather than as a common project of all. After all was settled, Germans renewed the Roman system of great estates that were worked by tenant farmers. With the coming of the Arab invasions, all commercial activity between Western Europe and the Middle East ceased. The result was to increase the trend toward agrarianism. The Byzantine Empire had kept up trade, but in the West, trade, when it existed, was localized around Italy.[1]

In the twenty-first century, the situation is somewhat different, but the caste system endures in certain ways. Hernando de Soto points out persuasively that in developing countries a caste system is created by government bureaucracy. He shows that in many countries, to be able to buy a house *legally* or start a business, sometimes years of bureaucratic office visits with their concomitant paperwork is necessary. For instance, in Peru, the process to obtain a home legally takes five stages, the first of which consists of 207 steps; in the Philippines, 168 steps, which takes between 13 to 25 years. In Egypt, to purchase desert land for construction takes 77 steps and requires 6 to 14 years; and, in Haiti, to obtain a sales contract following a five-year lease contract, it takes 111 steps and 4,112 days, which is 11.3 years.[2] The result of all this is that people have a disincentive to do any business or residential transactions legally and instead resort merely to exchanging cash for a house or business without ownership title. This creates a caste of formal and informal businesses. Those who buy homes informally risk having them taken away either by the government or by the original landowner should he show up with a title. De Soto points out:

> When these remedies [Western statist schemes for foreign aid] fail, westerners all too often respond not by questioning the adequacy of the remedies but by blaming Third World peoples for their lack of entrepreneurial spirit or market orientation. If they have failed to prosper despite all the excellent advice, it is because something is the

---

[1] Christine Rider, *Introduction to Economic History* (Cincinnati: South Western College Publishing, 1995), 20–24.

[2] Hernando de Soto, *The Mystery of Capital: Why Capitalism Triumphs in the West and Fails Everywhere Else* (New York: Basic Books, 2000), 22–27.

matter with them.... The cities of the Third World and the former communist countries are teeming with entrepreneurs. You cannot walk through a Middle Eastern market, hike up to a Latin American village, or climb into a taxicab in Moscow without someone trying to make a deal with you. The inhabitants of these countries possess talent, enthusiasm, and an *astonishing ability to wring a profit out of practically nothing*.[3]

The problem, according to De Soto, is that the governments, by their very overbearing bureaucratic requirements, cause capital to be hidden and unusable:

[T]he major stumbling block that keeps the rest of the world from benefiting from capitalism is its inability to produce capital. Capital is the force that raises the productivity of labor and creates the wealth of nations. It is the lifeblood of the capitalist system, the foundation of progress, and the one thing that the poor countries cannot seem to produce for themselves, no matter how eagerly their people engage in all the other activities that characterize a capitalist economy.[4]

All of this prohibits serious wealth creation.

It is peculiar that the Church's official documents hardly mention this problem. In neglecting this subject while focusing on the greed and other failings of businesspeople, the Church misses one of the largest systemic problems the remedy of which would make a severe dent in the poverty of the world.[5]

---

[3] De Soto, *The Mystery of Capital*, 3–4, my emphasis.

[4] De Soto, *The Mystery of Capital*, 5.

[5] See, for example, Pope Pius XI, *Quadragesimo Anno*, and Pope Benedict XVI, *Caritas in Veritate*. Pope John Paul II's *Centesimus Annus* is a notable exception to this characterization. For a thorough discussion of the origin and development of Catholic notions

After the eighth century, because of the invasions by Arabs and Vikings, trade died, cities and towns shrank, and the need for survival grew. Portable wealth disappeared, and political power came to depend completely on land. Now everything was decentralized because of the need for protection. As Rider states: "[T]he cost of this security was a surrender of liberty. But this cost was willingly paid—not to have done so implied only a freedom to starve, to be raped, looted, pillaged, and destroyed or enslaved."[6] The whole basis of the feudal system of the Middle Ages was the feudal contract made between a lord and his tenant. Each had duties to one another, and there were legal remedies for failure to attend to those duties.[7] Nevertheless, there was no way to escape one's social status. Large landholders possessed their lands by grant of the king, lower landholders by grant of their higher lords, and vassals by contract with the lord.[8] Even in communal villages, procedures for farming were strictly governed, and this "had direct practicable consequences

---

hostile to the market, see William R. Luckey, "The Intellectual Origins of Modern Catholic Social Teachings on Economics," https://www.scribd.com/document/105782660/William-Luckey; William R. Luckey, "The Crisis in Catholic Social Teaching on Economics" [paper given at *The Lew Church Memorial Lecture on Religion and Economics*, Austrian Scholars Conference, Auburn, Alabama (March 15, 2007)] (audio, MP3), https://mises.org/library/crisis-catholic-social-teaching-economics; and William R. Luckey, "Suggestions on Rebuilding Catholic Social Teachings on Economics," *Journal of the Institute of Economic Affairs* 30, no. 1 (2010): 30–31.

[6] Rider, *Economic History*, 25.

[7] Such as the *Assizes of Jerusalem*. See Joseph Costanzo, SJ, *Political and Legal Studies*, vol. 1, *Politeia* (West Hanover, MA: Christopher Publishing, 1982), 82–84.

[8] Sir Paul Vinogradoff, "Feudalism" in *The Cambridge Medieval History* (Cambridge: Cambridge University Press, 1968), 458–84.

in hampering private industry and the use of private capital in cultivation."⁹ Hence, wealth creation was virtually nonexistent.

Innovation in medieval times began with the introduction and widespread use of the wheeled plow. When the lighter, simpler, Roman plow was in use, the two-course system was used. Fields under this system were used and then left fallow in alternate years so that the soil could restore moisture and nutrients. This occurred mostly around the Mediterranean basin where there were long, dry summers and lighter soils. The kind of farming found in the Mediterranean area hardly appears in northwestern Europe, which focused on livestock grazing. Old Roman plows were unable to penetrate the rich, heavier soils of the area. But with widespread use of the wheeled plow pulled by oxen or draft animals, the harder soil was more easily cultivated; the heavy clods of clay and loam soils could now be broken up. Farmers were able to shift to a three-course rotation. Now one-third extra land could be planted with food crops, and the yields were larger per unit of labor and capital.

The result of this great innovation in farming was that more crops could be produced than just those needed by the tenants. This also meant that people could live in villages, and still be fed, or could travel and take food with them. The situation reversed itself when the towns and cities invented improvements in farming and sold them in the countryside, further increasing crop output.[10]

The Medieval Church's Response to Poverty

At this point, the stress of the Church was on helping those who suffered through the vicissitudes of fortune, whether famine, storm, pests, or disease. Wealthy persons were encouraged to

---

[9] Vinogradoff, "Feudalism," 474.
[10] Jane Jacobs, *The Economy of Cities* (New York: Vintage, 1970).

give of their substance to those in such situations.[11] In this case, *substance* meant mostly food. In the countryside, it fell to the lord to take care of the poor. In towns and cities, the bishop was responsible, and this responsibility was decentralized to the parishes, with the deacons and arch-priests or merely parish priests actually doing the work. Due care had to be taken to prevent fraud, which is why giving money was strongly discouraged. Lists of the poor were kept, and the family receiving aid was shielded from any opprobrium as a result of their penury. The Church virtually invented the hospital, staffed by religious orders whose duty was to care for the sick-poor. The Church also saw itself as having a duty of giving spiritual advice and moral teaching to the poor so that they did not learn to depend on the assistance given them, or become lazy, trying to avoid work because the food would keep coming.[12] This approach to charity, rich in spiritual and material wisdom, can be seen throughout the Church's history in the lives of the great saints of charity. Among the best known is St. Vincent de Paul (1581–1660), who embodied the best Church policies toward the poor.

Finally, the medieval Church also tried to find ways to prevent conditions that fostered poverty, though the Church was vague about what those ways were. Some concerned the prevention of usury, which did not apply much to the lowest classes of society because, for the most part, the lower classes did not participate in borrowing money.[13] It turns out that the Church's prohibition of charging interest on a loan had the effect of stifling many business enterprises and giving Jews and Lombards a monopoly on loans, thereby, as in the case of so

---

[11] Guy Bedouelle, OP, *St. Dominic: The Grace of the Word* (San Francisco: Ignatius Press, 1987), 19–29.

[12] "Care of the Poor by the Church," *The Catholic Encyclopedia*, accessed June 15, 2010, http://www.newadvent.org/cathen/12236a.htm.

[13] "Care of the Poor by the Church," *The Catholic Encyclopedia*.

many monopolies, allowing the interest rates to be inflated.[14] Obviously, however, the high monopoly-interest rates must have not been so high as to cause the majority of borrowers to default, and they had to be low enough for them to attract customers. In addition, contrary to the popular concept of monopolies, the threat of other lenders coming in to take market share would be enough to compel the interest rates to be lower than one might expect, so as to discourage possible competitors. It is also wrong to see the Jewish and Lombard moneylenders as two single companies. Within those groups were individual lenders who competed with each other.

The Church's prohibition of usury is interesting in light of the parable of the talents (Matt. 25:14–30). Here our Lord says to the unprofitable servant who hid his talent in the earth: "Then you ought to have invested my money with the bankers, and at my coming I should have received what was my own with interest" (Matt. 25:27). Would our Lord give an example of someone doing something that was morally questionable to illustrate a good thing, even though the parable is about not wasting the gifts of God?[15]

---

[14] *The New Catholic Encyclopedia*, 2nd ed., 2003, *s.v.* "Usury."

[15] See a discussion on the effects of usury on banking and the "Depositum Confessatum" in Jesús Huerta de Soto, *Money, Bank Credit and Economic Cycles* (Auburn, AL: Mises Institute, 2006), 64–69.

IV The Beginning of Wealth Creation

What brought about the demise of feudalism? Besides the wheeled plow, another important factor was the use of money. Money facilitates exchange. Picture a crop farmer in the old days who wanted to get some milk or beef to feed himself and his family. He would have to drag his corn around to dairy farm after dairy farm until he found enough farmers who were willing to exchange corn for milk or beef. This would not only be sheer drudgery but also time consuming. At some point in time—it may have varied by culture—people started exchanging something that everyone wanted to have for the things that they needed. For Native Americans, it was strings of colored stones and shells (wampum). For the natives of an island in the Pacific Ocean, it was large stones (whose ownership rather than physical possession changed, since they were too big to haul around). Roman soldiers carried bags of salt with them to exchange for things they needed from a place they were passing through. In Rome, cows were frequently used as a medium of exchange. Gradually, in societies that were advancing, people settled on precious metals such as gold and silver.[1] These metals had many

---

[1] This is called the Monetary Regression Theorem. It was developed by Carl Menger, *Principles of Economics* (1871; repr., New York: New York University Press, 1981), 257. See also Ludwig von Mises, *The Theory of Money and Credit* (1912; repr., Indianapolis: Liberty Classics, 1980), 42–49.

uses, were malleable, easy to carry, and measurable by weight. People wanted them as commodities; for instance, for jewelry and decoration. The result was that wealth could now travel. Instead of carrying foodstuffs to exchange, one could carry a commonly accepted precious metal. Note that government had no hand in choosing what would be used as a medium of exchange. When rulers put their face stamp on a coin, it acted as a guarantee that the metal was worth what it said it was, although rulers found ways to circumvent this all the time.[2]

Now, couple the use of precious metals as a medium of exchange with the surplus of food now being produced. A person could travel and take both food and coins with him. If this traveler was near a port, he could take a large amount of food with him and trade it to the ships from the East for the contents of the ships. The traveler could then take those items back to his community. Once there, he would open a booth where people would come, view the things he had brought back from port, and purchase them with precious metals or with direct exchange of commodities. This was the origin of the medieval bazaars, which later developed into towns. Notice that all of this is spontaneous. Once more food was produced, more mobility was allowed. More mobility allowed for the division of labor, which required specialization. Specialization and the division of labor were very important for the betterment of civilization. Adam Smith writes of the origins of the division of labor as follows: "The greatest improvement in the productive powers of labor, and the greater part of the skill, dexterity, and judgment which it is any where directed, or applied, seem to be the effects of the division of labor."[3]

---

[2] See Ludwig von Mises, "The Origin of Money," in *The Theory of Money and Credit* (New Haven: Yale University Press, 1953), 41–46.

[3] Adam Smith, *An Inquiry into the Nature and Causes of the Wealth of Nations* (1976; repr., Indianapolis: Liberty Press, 1981), 3. Note:

Smith explains the source of the division of labor:

> This division of labor, from which so many advantages are derived, is not originally the effect of any human wisdom, which foresees and intends that general opulence to which it gives occasion. It is a necessary, though very slow and gradual consequence of a certain propensity in human nature which has in view no such extensive utility; the propensity to truck, barter and exchange.[4]

Smith illustrates the results of the division of labor with his observations in a pin factory. If one man had to do all the operations in making the pin, he might produce one pin per day, and certainly not as many as twenty. But if the operations were distributed, where one man stretched the wire, another cut it, another formed the head, and so forth (eighteen distinct operations), eighteen men could produce forty-eight thousand pins per day.[5]

But why would one want to make forty-eight thousand pins? Well, this brings us to another economic principle enunciated by Smith: the division of labor can only go as far as the extent of the market. The larger the market, the more people there are who will purchase a product or service. Large cities have greater markets than small towns. In the pin example, given the small number of pins made without the division of labor

---

Adam Smith was not an economist but a professor of moral philosophy. He wrote this book because he considered the state-run economy of mercantilism, in operation at the time, as immoral because it kept the people poor and the rulers rich. Mercantilism was a major cause of the American War of Independence.

[4] Smith, *An Inquiry into the Nature and Causes of the Wealth of Nations*, 25. The propensity to truck, barter and exchange comes from human reason, Smith says.

[5] Smith, *An Inquiry into the Nature and Causes of the Wealth of Nations*, 14–15.

and the large number of pins demanded by homemakers and tailors in their sewing, the cost of each pin would be comparatively high. Poor people could not afford expensive pins, so they would forgo purchasing new pins and make do with what they already have. Only the well-off can afford new pins because they have to bid for the pins, thus pushing the price up. But if the factory makes forty-eight thousand pins in a day, the supply becomes greater, and people do not have to bid for pins because the distributer does not want to be stuck with thousands of pins (pardon the pun) that he already paid the factory for. Hence, he lowers the price so that all the pins get sold. The division of labor has done its job by increasing the market for pins and allowing more people to have them.

This is how civilizations achieve a better quality of life. Returning to our medieval example, we see that as the Middle Ages progress, people are better fed due to the invention and then later the widespread use of the wheeled plow. Travel begins to take place, and people gain experience by seeing how other people do things. Trade occurs out of the district or even at seaports, giving people at home the opportunity to acquire knives and forks, better plows, medicines, and clothing—things that better their lives. Even the wealthier folks such as the lords would purchase extravagant and expensive things: tapestries, spices from the east, and coffee, for instance. With the widespread use of money, people do not have to take things to the bazaars to trade for other things brought in by merchants. Instead, they take coins, which the sellers of various items can store up as capital to use later and to better their own lives and those of their families.

Now, with better living conditions, life expectancy increased and child mortality declined. One proof of this lies in world population figures. Data shows that the world population increased very slowly (about one percent per hundred years) throughout most of human history, and then began accelerating rapidly in the early modern era (seventeenth century). During the late twentieth century, the rate was more than 250 percent per hundred years.[6]

This tremendous increase in population was due to increases in food, sanitation, clothing, medicines, and other items that foster human flourishing. The availability of these goods was in turn due to the gradual growth of a market economy, and, especially in later times, wealth creation. Without this increase in wealth, early death rates would still be high due to poor diets, inadequate medical care, and low quality of life in general.

This slow and spontaneous growth in wealth creation continued until fairly recent times, when the process itself began to be questioned by writers such as Karl Marx who portrayed factory owners as greedy people, repressing the workers by paying subsistence wages while they kept almost all the profits.[7] Even Catholic leaders such as Bishop Wilhelm von Ketteler accepted this notion and influenced other Catholic thinkers.[8] These thinkers failed to take adequate account of the challenge and significance of creating wealth.

---

[6] Julian L. Simon, *The State of Humanity* (Oxford: Blackwell, 1995), 8–9.

[7] This was all based on the "wage fund doctrine" accepted erroneously by almost all the classical economists (see discussion in chapter 5).

[8] See *The Social Teachings of Wilhelm Emmanuel von Ketteler, Bishop of Mainz (1811–1877)*, ed. by Rupert J. Ederer (Washington, DC: University Press of America, 1981), 321.

V The Contemporary View of the Church: The Special Case of *Populorum Progressio*

The social teaching of the Church, as expressed in Pope Leo XIII's *Rerum Novarum* (1891) and subsequent papal encyclicals, is a serious and insightful reflection on social and economic matters rooted in the natural law and Christian doctrine. Catholic social teaching has done much to promote the dignity of the person, the value of labor, and sound understanding of the importance and character of private property.

As some observers have noted, however, there are gaps and weaknesses in this body of social teaching. One of these is a failure to take into account the achievement of wealth creation described in chapters 1–4 of this book and to explore the sources of that achievement. This blind spot has, at times, led to inadequate appreciation of the benefits of free markets. The trend of skepticism regarding the free market and its ability to create wealth continued with *Populorum Progressio*, issued by Pope Paul VI in 1967. The period when Paul wrote was the heyday of Keynesian economics, especially in government circles. (Despite extensive discussion among economists of the flaws in his system, John Maynard Keynes's picture appeared on the December 31, 1965, edition of *Time* magazine, twenty-nine years after the publication of his *General Theory of Employment, Interest, and Money*, and nineteen years after his death.) Keynes's approach to economic development was artificial stimulation of the economy through government spending and expansion of the money supply.[1] If, said many economists who accepted Keynes's theory without serious examination, a faltering domestic economy can be bettered by injections of money through government deficit spending, then it follows that in underdeveloped countries an injection of money by the wealthier countries would accomplish the same thing. Thus, the best way to help developing countries is to give them foreign aid.

This Keynesian approach appears to be the one favored by Pope Paul VI. At the heart of this approach is the idea that wealth creation and wealth distribution can be separated. This notion was originally introduced by John Stuart Mill in *Principles of Political Economy* (1848). Mill does a decent job of explaining the creation of wealth, but he does not see the distribution of wealth as part of the wealth creation system:

> Even what a person has produced by his individual toil, unaided by any one, he cannot keep, unless by permission of society. Not only can society take it from him, but individuals could and would take it from him, if society only remained passive; if it did not either interfere *en mass*, or employ and pay people for the purpose of preventing him from being disturbed in the possession.... [Therefore], [s]ociety can subject the distribution of wealth to what ever rules it thinks best; but what practical results will flow from the operation of those rules, must be discovered, like any other physical or mental truths, by observation and reasoning.[2]

---

[1] John Maynard Keynes, *The General Theory of Employment, Interest and Money* (London: Macmillan, 1936), 326.

[2] John Stuart Mill, *Principles of Political Economy* (1848), II.1.2. Available online at http://www.econlib.org/library/Mill/mlP.html.

Basically, to Mill, the production of wealth not only has nothing to do with the distribution of it—in other words, how it gets to the people—but society can decide how it is to be distributed on a kind of trial and error basis.

To understand this principle, we must go back to the classical economists' view of the "iron law of wages" that was in turn based on both the "labor theory of value" and the "wage fund doctrine."

The *labor theory of value* said that the value of a good came from the amount of labor hours put in to the making of the good. Hence, a good that took ten hours to make should get twice as much return in sale as one that took only five hours.

The *wage fund doctrine* held that employers had a fund with which to pay workers. Because they did not want to give away all of their money, they gave the workers only enough to induce them to come to work. Any less and they would not have the energy to work; any more and they would work one day and stay home the next, having made enough money to tide them over.[3] This is the origin of the idea of the exploitation of workers. The workers, many said, are not getting what they are worth, judged by the labor theory of value, and the employers are keeping the surplus (the theory of surplus value). If this were true, it would be truly unjust.

The *iron law of wages* said that workers are forever stuck in this exploitive situation. They get a break if the population declines, for then the employers must pay more to bid workers away from other employers. Then, as a result of workers' eating and living better, the population increases, and wages will decline because of the surplus of available workers.

The Reverend Thomas Malthus, an Anglican clergyman, applied this theory to food production. He theorized that popu-

---

[3] See the discussion of "theory X" and "theory Y" in Douglas McGregor, *The Human Side of Enterprise* (New York: McGraw-Hill, 1960), pt. 1.

lation grows geometrically (e.g., 2 x 2 x 2) while the food supply increases arithmetically (e.g., 2 + 2 + 2). Population increase would eventually outrun the food supply. This food shortage would cause a decline in population, and then people would eat better, which would lead to a population increase, and the cycle would repeat. In any case, food supplies would hover around bare subsistence.[4]

Because it is true, according to the above theories, that the factory owners are hoarding their wealth by paying a bare subsistence wage,[5] the problem is how to get the money out of the owners' hands and into the workers' hands. This is the problem of distribution.

Most proposals favor a "tax the rich" solution. It is argued that the rich are holding on to their wealth and depriving the workers of their just wage based on the labor theory of value. Therefore, the state must take it from them by taxation; hence, the call for the graduated income tax. Under this scheme, the more money one makes, the more money one should pay, not only in absolute terms (for example, 10 percent of $5,000 is $500,

---

[4] Malthus is the father of population control in international economics. It should be noted, however, that Malthus never recommended artificial birth control but instead methods such as postponing marriage.

[5] Notice how Pope Pius XI states it:

> Property, that is "capital" has undoubtedly long been able to appropriate too much to itself. Whatever was produced, whatever returns accrued, capital claimed for itself, leaving to the worker hardly enough to restore and renew his strength. For the doctrine was preached that all accumulation of capital falls by an insuperable economic law to the rich, and that by the same law, the workers are given over and bound to perpetual want, to the scantiest of livelihoods. *Quadragesimo Anno*, no. 54.

A better summary of the "iron law of wages" would be hard to find.

but 10 percent of $50,000 is $5,000) but also in a higher percentage (30 percent of $50,000 is $15,000). Karl Marx advocated such a tax. "The proletariat will use its political supremacy [in the dictatorship of the proletariat, after the overthrow of the capitalists] to wrest, by degrees, all capital from the bourgeoisie [by] … a heavy or progressive or graduated income tax."[6]

Now, not all those who have suggested the graduated income tax are trying to "wrest all capital from the bourgeoisie." In fact, it is now the case that most income earners paying the higher brackets of graduated tax rates are not employers at all but employees themselves, so that Marx's original justification is no longer relevant. Still, it is instructive to remember that the iron law of wages was one of the intellectual sources for the progressive income tax.

We clearly see in the above ideas the assumptions that "capitalists" are very good at producing wealth and that they have no reason to distribute it.[7] What is missing is serious discussion of wealth creation or economic development. The Keynesian and Marxist approaches seem to see the world as a static-sized pie; some have ended up with bigger slices and some with smaller slices. Those who hold the larger slices refuse to share theirs with those who have very small ones, like children who have not learned the value of sharing.

In *Populorum Progressio*, Paul VI says he wants to help bring about a more humane world. One of the ways he proposes to do so is by mitigating the evils of "liberal capitalism," thus invoking a theme common in earlier social encyclicals. One of the principal difficulties of interpreting the popes' writings on

---

[6] Karl Marx, *The Manifesto of the Communist Party*, in Robert C. Tucker, ed., *The Marx-Engels Reader*, 2nd ed. (New York: W. W. Norton, 1978), 490.

[7] See the treatment of this idea in Pius XI, *Quadragesimo Anno*, nos. 56–58.

economics is understanding the meaning of terms that denote different things to different readers. One of these problematic terms is *capitalism*. Saint John Paul II explicitly recognized this difficulty in *Centesimus Annus* when he identified two different meanings of capitalism, each of which would elicit different judgments from the Church.[8] It is important to keep this problem in mind as we consider what the popes have written concerning economic matters.

In *Populorum*, Pope Paul VI distinguishes industrialization, which he considers good, from the system of capitalism that accompanied it.

> But if it is true that a type of capitalism has been the source of excessive suffering, injustices and fratricidal conflicts whose effects still persist, it would also be wrong to attribute to industrialization itself evils that belong to the woeful system which *accompanied* it. On the contrary one must recognize in all justice the irreplaceable contribution made by the organization of labour and of industry to what development has accomplished.[9]

For Pope Paul, it would seem that industrialism grew up on its own and capitalism had nothing to do with it. Capitalism, instead, was a system that developed independently and that was created to enable—or at least developed in such a way that it permits—the exploitation of those who lack economic resources. If this is true then, *mutatis mutandis*, economic development should be carried on independently of the capitalistic mindset that caused it in the first place. To this end, Paul VI emphasizes, without excluding private initiatives, government programs that "are necessary in order 'to encourage, stimulate, co-ordinate,

---

[8] See John Paul II, *Centesimus Annus*, no. 42.
[9] Paul VI, *Populorum Progressio*, no. 26, emphasis added.

supplement and integrate'"[10] the activity of individuals and of intermediary bodies.[11] Further: "It pertains to the public authorities to choose, *even to lay down* the objectives to be pursued, the ends to be achieved, and the means for attaining these, and it is for them to stimulate all the forces engaged in this common activity."[12] Importantly, the pope adds a caveat: "But let them [the public authorities] associate private initiative and intermediary bodies with this work. They will thus avoid the danger of complete collectivization or of arbitrary planning which, by denying liberty, would prevent the exercise of the fundamental rights of the human person."[13]

Paul's proposal here raises a serious problem. Notice that his focus is necessarily on places where there are successful, wealthy people, which means mostly Western-style economies (Europe, North America, Hong Kong, and Japan). How does one let public authorities choose and even force the objectives and the means to achieve them without trampling the legitimate freedom of the human person? How does one do this without killing the incentives for economic projects?

Legitimate is an important word here because there are certain things that all agree are illegitimate. Discrimination based on race or national origin, for instance, and leaving aside questions of identification and enforcement, is illegal (as well as economically destructive[14]). Not paying workers what they deserve is illegal, at least in the West. Stealing from the employer is illegal. These things are illegal because society, through the instrument of the political system, has expressed its view that they are

---

[10] Paul VI is quoting Pope John XXIII's *Mater et Magistra*.

[11] Paul VI, *Populorum Progressio*, no. 33.

[12] Paul VI, *Populorum Progressio*, emphasis added.

[13] Paul VI, *Populorum Progressio*.

[14] Gary S. Becker, *The Economics of Discrimination* (Chicago: University of Chicago Press, 1971).

immoral *and* damaging enough to merit punishment.[15] These legal prohibitions are operational requirements in states where capitalism flourishes. Why? Because they are necessary for the free market to flourish. How did they become law? Not because everybody in the capitalist system violates the morality behind them but because there are always those who try to cut corners. It is part of our fallen nature. The same is true concerning the enforcement of contracts. Of all the people with whom a business makes deals, the vast majority will honor the agreements; but some *might* not. The business does not know who these are, so it makes a contract with everybody to protect itself from the one or two who might not honor their agreements. If no one kept their agreements, life in society would be miserable.

The Nobel Prize-winning economist James Buchanan explains it this way:

> Contractual obligation, expressed by the willingness of individuals to behave in accordance with specified terms, depends critically on explicit or imagined participation. Individuals, having "given their word," are "honor bound" to live up to the terms. This remains true even if, subsequent to agreement, these terms come to be viewed as "unfair," or "unjust." Defection or violation runs counter to widely accepted moral codes for personal behavior.[16]

Of course, if the culture does not recognize the obligation of persons to keep their word, then agreements and contracts

---

[15] Note that society does not punish all immoral actions, only those that noticeably harm the common good. See St. Thomas, *S. Th.*, q. 96, a. 2.

[16] James Buchanan, *The Collected Works of James M. Buchanan*, vol. 7, *The Limits of Liberty: Between Anarchy and Leviathan* (Indianapolis: Liberty Fund, 2000), 96–97.

become "shackles" and oppressive.[17] In the case of widespread moral degeneration, even contracts will not prevent many people from violating their word, and this situation will effectively kill trust, which is necessary to make long-term agreements. The Catholic political philosopher Bertrand de Jouvenel shows how society must have trust as its basis:

> Human actions are, it is clear, based on confidence in others. The condition of a man would be miserable—it might be truer to say that he never would have become a man—if at every moment he had to be on guard against the unforeseeable actions of every other man. Our progress toward the human condition presupposes that we live in a circle of peace and friendship, in which we not only do not anticipate attacks but we expect to be succored at need.[18]

Can a free market function without the underlying culture of morality regarding the obligation of keeping one's word? Phrased differently, can a free market exist without trust? No. Look at cultures that are founded on dissimulation and fraud. Entrepreneurs in these places are limited to selling the wares that they made at home, such as baskets and clay pots, at booths. Any higher level of production requires long-term, distant relations with suppliers, and in such a culture neither the suppliers nor the business customer can be trusted to fulfill their end of the bargain. For example, the supplier might not send the correct product, or the business customer might not pay for the goods once shipped. Under these conditions, the court system is also corrupt and functions according to bribes that not everyone can

---

[17] Bertrand de Jouvenel, *Sovereignty: An Inquiry into the Political Good* (1957; repr., Indianapolis: Liberty Fund, 1997), 321.

[18] Bertrand de Jouvenel, *Sovereignty*, 137.

afford, which makes the legal system no place to go for justice. As a result, there is no serious economic development.

Another problem with Pope Paul's *Populorum Progressio*, with its apparently heavy reliance on the intervention of government, is its foundational assumption that in reality government has the common good in mind. It is one thing to look at government metaphysically to see that it is created by God, is necessary to society, and is supposed to act for the common good. In practice, however, there is another story. All men act in their own self-interest. This is not a bad thing, and is not to be equated, except in rare cases, with selfishness.[19] Many of my acts for my own self-interest help the common good. Getting an education, eating, working—the last of which produces things and services others need—and bringing home a paycheck to support my family, all enhance the common good. At the same time, there are many kinds of actions that harm the common good in large or small ways. People constantly make choices between actions that promote or actions that harm the common good.

---

[19] Some commentators distort Adam Smith's notion about self-interest to mean pure, unadulterated selfishness. Smith uses the term *self-love*, but means it clearly in a more biblical sense, that we must love our neighbors *as ourselves*. This means we must do our daily duty to support ourselves and our families. An exchange works on the principle that we interest a person in doing something because it will benefit that person. To ask a person to do something that will only benefit me, is called a *favor*, not an exchange. The economic term for the more selfish aspects of economics is "rent seeking," and it usually happens in government or when there is a collusion of government and companies. A rent is obtained when an entity, whether politician or business or both together extract money from someone else, while not giving them anything in return, as when companies importune governments to grant monopoly privileges. See Jac C. Hackelman, ed., *Readings in Public Choice Economics* (Ann Arbor: University of Michigan Press, 2004), sec. 1, "Rent Seeking."

Examples include deciding to publish either a news magazine or a pornographic one, or selling either hot dogs or crack. The person's own sense of morality would help him to make the right choice, but the lucrativeness of the wrong choice might push him to the wrong one.

People's tendency to act in their own self-interest applies to government officials as well. The *government* does not do anything; that is the fallacy of reification. *People* in the government do things. The idea that government officials act for the common good, or do "public service," is generally a myth, especially on the margins where their positions on issues would cause them to lose an election, or forfeit a job in the bureaucracy: "[P]oliticians on occasion vote for things that they think are right rather than things which will help them get re-elected … this is a relatively minor activity compared to maximizing one's own well-being."[20]

Saint Augustine had very strong views on this subject, and he was no friend of government.[21] For Augustine, there are citizens of two cities mixed together in this world. They are citizens of the earthly city or citizens of the heavenly city, depending on

---

[20] Gordon Tullock, *The Selected Works of Gordon Tullock*, vol. 1, *Virginia Political Economy* (Indianapolis: Liberty Fund, 2004), 16. One economist who thinks that this theory is too mild is Robert Higgs who thinks that it is the ruthless who get power, and that "doing the right thing" is really throwing the people a bone as they do their power- and money-seeking activities. See Robert Higgs, "Public Choice and Political Leadership," chap. 5, in *Against Leviathan: Government Power and the Free Society* (Oakland, CA: Independent Institute, 2004).

[21] See the discussion in Herbert A. Dean, *The Social and Political Ideas of St. Augustine* (New York: Columbia University Press, 1963), chap. 4. Interestingly, Pope Benedict XVI has a great love for St. Augustine's thought, but nonetheless displays a great trust in government in *Caritas in Veritate*.

the objects of their love. The citizens of the City of God love God even to contempt of self, and the citizens of the earthly city love themselves even to contempt of God,[22] but the citizens of both cities dwell together on this earth. Governments, in Augustine's view, are usually controlled by the citizens of the earthly city who have only their own interest at heart. He spends a large part of the *City of God* describing the atrocities perpetrated by those misdirected citizens, beginning with Cain's killing of Abel, after which Cain founded the first city. To Augustine, the only function of government that is legitimate is the protection of the citizens of the City of God from the citizens of the earthly city.

Why would citizens of the earthly city be willing to cooperate in such protection? Their own self-interest. In order to stay in power and gain support for their personal aims, they have to protect the generality of citizens, both man-centered and God-centered. If those who love God are not protected, the self-centered cannot be sure that the rulers will protect them either. One cannot expect justice or virtue from rulers, except on occasion when a good ruler is in power. Such a ruler often incurs the wrath of vicious citizens, however, in which case he may be exiled or even assassinated. In any case, he eventually passes from the scene, and it is back to the old ways.[23]

Keeping this discussion in mind, we consider Pope Paul's recommendation that both privately contributed and public funds be increased so that people can be freed not only from the destitution imposed by others but also from the circumstances beyond the control of the poor person. His aim is a world where

---

[22] St. Augustine, *The City of God*, bk. 14, chap. 28.

[23] Cicero is a good example of this. A great thinker, he was called on to be Consul of Rome twice but was killed on order of Marcus Antonius, and his head and his hands were nailed to the podium in the forum.

every man ... can live a fully human life ... a world where freedom is not an empty word and where the poor man Lazarus can sit down at the same table with the rich man. This demands great generosity, much sacrifice and unceasing effort on the part of the rich man.... Is he prepared to support out of his own pocket works and undertakings organized in favour of the most destitute? Is he ready to pay higher taxes so that the public authorities can intensify their efforts in favor of development? Is he ready to pay a higher price for imported goods so that the producer may be more justly rewarded?[24]

It is a bit of a challenge to sort out exactly which measures the pope is recommending here. His call for the wealthy to sacrifice and to strive so as to make possible the economic development of the poor is unobjectionable. As has already been noted, the fact that wealth carries such obligations has been a constant theme in Christian teaching from the early fathers through the scholastics to modern Catholic social teaching.

It is also clear at the end of this passage, however, that the pope is calling for government involvement in the promotion of development. Paul does not specify what he has in mind, but the exhortation may be (and has normally been) interpreted to mean government-to-government grants, commonly denoted as *foreign aid*. In retrospect, the wisdom of this recommendation must be called into question—not because the principle of the Christian obligation to help those in need is problematic, but because the track record of foreign aid is dubious on the very terms of its own intended purpose (i.e., to foster economic development in poor nations). Thomas Woods's critique is apropos:

> There [in *Populorum Progressio*] the Pope called for the very kind of Western-funded Third World development

---

[24] Paul VI, *Populorum Progressio*, 47.

programmes that have proved so disastrous in practice. These programmes—as scholars such as Peter Bauer pointed out in vain at the time—served to prop up some of the most brutal regimes in the world, and shielded dictators from the full consequences of their destructive economic policies. They delayed necessary economic reforms, enlarged the state sector at the expense of the productive economy, and created often violent ethnic and racial tension as competing groups scrambled to gain control of the state apparatus in order to control western grant money. The encyclical was filled with the standard criticisms of the free market, yet it was the most market-oriented of the less developed nations that wound up prospering the most, and where the lot of the poor improved most dramatically.[25]

The social teaching of the Church has itself developed on this matter. As Philip Booth has noted, the writings of Benedict XVI on foreign aid, if not entirely negative, are nonetheless much more cautious than Paul's endorsements. Benedict highlights the dangers of government assistance, pointing to some of the same problems to which Woods draws attention in the quotation above.[26]

---

[25] Thomas E. Woods, Jr., "The Unanswered Questions of the Just Wage," in *Catholic Social Teaching and the Market Economy*, ed. Philip Booth (London: Institute of Economic Affairs, 2007), 95. For a biography and evaluation of the work of the above-mentioned P. T. Bauer, see http://www.elcato.org/special/friedman/bauer/yamey.pdf, accessed, July 22, 2010. See also Peter Bauer, "The Disregard of Reality," in *The Revolution in Development Economics* (Washington, DC: Cato Institute, 1998), 25–39.

[26] Philip Booth, *International Aid and Integral Human Development* (Grand Rapids: Acton Institute, 2011); see esp. chap. 4.

VI   The Science of the Creation and Distribution of Wealth

What is the scientific basis for the creation of wealth? Start with Carl Menger's definition of a good. When an Austrian economist speaks of a *good*, he is not necessarily speaking of tangible goods such as a washing machine or a car. For Menger and others influenced by the Aristotelian-Thomistic tradition, a good is that which we believe is *good*—anything that will satisfy a need that a person has. This good is seen in a subjective sense, which is a contribution of the phenomenological viewpoint. There are objective goods in the universe, but to desire this or that objectively good *good*, I must subjectivize it; that is, I must actually see it as a good for me at this particular time.[1]

The needs that people experience can be almost anything: education, love, food, culture, or the above-mentioned washing machine. There are two types of goods for our purposes: free goods, that is, things that are part of our natural environment and that we can have whenever we want, such as air; and economic goods, that is, goods of which there are not enough to satisfy our desires. Because our desires have no real limit, and economic goods are finite, the latter must be economized.

---

[1] Aristotle makes the distinction between real and apparent goods. Our fallen human nature tricks us into selecting the apparent ones often enough.

This means that they cannot be handed out indiscriminately, because the supply would vanish quickly. Remember, we are talking about anything that fills a human want, both tangible goods such as a car and intangible goods such as Byron's poetry.

Because human beings are not disembodied spirits, all goods are connected with the physical. The intangible satisfaction of hearing a Bach sonata relies on the availability of the physical sound waves that convey the music. One must trade something to hear the music; for example, buy a ticket to a concert hall where the sonata will be performed or buy a stereo system and a CD on which the sonata is recorded. However, note that the satisfaction gained by hearing the sonata will decrease in proportion to hearing the sonata such that a person might not want to hear it again after the one hundredth time listening to it on the CD. This means that to achieve more cultural satisfaction, one must purchase another, different CD. Our pursuit of such goods, if they are used properly, will take us closer to the ultimate Good—God. Only in him who is "the good," is satisfaction complete.

Most of the time, the goods we need are down-to-earth items such as food, clothing, and shelter. We need cars to get to work, to the store, and to church. We need medical and dental care, books to read, paper to write on, jewelry, deodorant, and the like. The connection of these goods and the good is sometimes hard to see. Why jewelry or deodorant? These things make life less burdensome, more beautiful, and more enjoyable for us and for those around us. It is good for women to feel that their appearance is appealing; jewelry contributes to that goal.[2] It is good to be considerate of others by minimizing unpleasant

---

[2] The example of jewelry is further illustrative of the dual character of many goods. While jewelry can serve the genuine good of persons as described here, it can also be the object of illegitimate desire; for example, when being worn merely for the purpose of

odors; deodorant serves that purpose. Are jewelry and deodorant necessary for life? No. Do they make life better? Yes.

In fact, since man is co-creator with God, as Pope John Paul II said,[3] he creates his own society that will serve his ends, most of which are only intermediate ends that should, in turn, serve his ultimate end. Hence, society, and the economy are spontaneous orders driven by the things human beings need. The novel *Robinson Crusoe* is a good example. Crusoe finds himself on an island, alone, with virtually nothing for his survival. He immediately begins to provide for his first necessity, food, and then other needs such as shelter. When Friday shows up, he makes arrangements with him to develop things that make life somewhat easier.[4] The more complex this society becomes, the more things are available to enhance human flourishing. In the novel, Crusoe finds a Bible among the ship's material, becomes a Christian, and then converts Friday. As life progresses, the social and economic relationships tend to higher things; for instance, one's eternal salvation.

The Motivation to Better Our Condition

What does it mean to say that we wish to "better" our lives? It is natural for human beings to want to bring themselves and their families to a state of affairs that is better than the present one. It does not matter if one speaks of finances, education, health, religion, or living conditions. People generally try to move to

---

displaying opulence (i.e., used as an instrument of conspicuous consumption).

[3] See John Paul II, *Laborem Exercens*, 12–13; and John Paul II, "Biblical Account of Creation Analyzed," in *Original Unity of Man and Woman: Catechesis on the Book of Genesis* (Boston: St. Paul Editions, 1981), 22.

[4] Murray Rothbard, *Man, Economy and the State with Power and Market* (Auburn, AL: Ludwig von Mises Institute, 2004), 47.

a better situation in all these areas and many more. If a person were completely content with his current state of affairs, that person would not do anything to change it. But people and life are dynamic, not static, and even sitting in a chair at your favorite beach can get old after a couple of hours. So you go indoors or swim in the waters. Even if you remain in the chair, you will shift your weight occasionally for the sake of comfort.

The effort to better one's state of affairs requires belief in cause and effect. One must be able to predict, *ceteris paribus*, that there are actions that will bring about a better state of affairs. In addition, there must be the possibility of performing those actions. In many underdeveloped countries, options are constrained for various reasons, diminishing the likelihood that people will (or can) better their conditions. In the West and places like it (Hong Kong, Taiwan, Singapore, and Japan), actions are usually available. In these places, there may be other reasons that people do not strive to better their condition, including apathy and the existence of perverse incentives (a weakening of the cause-and-effect relationship that normally motivates action).

When considering strategies for increasing wealth, then, this natural human drive to better one's condition is the engine that must be fueled. Approaches and policies that diminish this drive or redirect it in fruitless ways will end up being counterproductive. Without this natural drive to better our condition, the world would never have risen out of barbarism. If we destroy it, the world may turn back in that direction.

What Is Wealth?

Menger defines *property* as "the entire sum of goods at a person's command." He defines *wealth* as, "the entire sum of goods at an economizing person's command, the quantities of which are smaller than the requirements for them."[5] Contrary to what one often hears about "the wealthy" (those who are born with or inherit a lot of money), in a free-market system, those with money usually created it themselves. Remember, too, that wealth includes the intangible—the entire sum of things perceived as good by the person possessing them. Suppose the question was asked, "Were St. Dominic and St. Ignatius of Loyola wealthy?" The person equating wealth with money would answer, "No." According to Menger's definition, however, they *were* wealthy because they both had an immense number of goods in Menger's sense of the term. Both of them were among the most educated men of their time. Both had tremendous energy and drive. Both had cultivated a tremendous prayer life. And both had an insatiable desire to save souls. All of these—even the energy—had to be developed by the two saints. There are some folks who are energetic by nature, but can these people be energetic in the face of extreme want, cold, rejection, or desperation? This takes great character and dedication, both of which must be intentionally cultivated by long years of self-renunciation.

Because human beings have a daily duty to provide for themselves and their families, the intangible goods we have can be exchanged for tangible goods that we need to better our state of affairs. Consider the case of the present author. Once he had decided to go to graduate school and get his doctorate, he was beginning to exchange his active intellect and his desire to better the social order into a credential that would make him more likely to be able to do so, *and* support a family. Certainly, teaching in Catholic colleges is not a way to get rich in monetary terms, but it pays enough to live a modest life, enabling him to increase the wealth of society. He spread his learning to others, both in the classroom and by lecturing and publishing scholarly

---

[5] Carl Menger, *Principles of Economics* (1871; repr. New York: New York University Press, 1976), 109, Menger's emphasis.

articles and books. In return, he gets psychic benefits—the love of the profession, the fascination of learning, and making a difference in people's lives. The wealth increase in society is seen in both tangible and intangible goods. Taking his classes and reading his writings, hopefully, will better the persons and possibly allow those persons to better their state of affairs, intellectually and financially. The onus is on the students or readers or hearers to take what he teaches them and act to change their state of affairs. As St. James said regarding the gospel: "For if any one is a hearer of the word and not a doer, he is like a man who observes his natural face in a mirror; for he observes himself and goes away and at once forgets what he was like" (James 1:23–24). Even the persons with no real skills can do something to better their lives just by the fact that they can think and move.

As was pointed out, many have argued that the free-market system is good at the production of wealth but not at the distribution of wealth. This claim makes the assumption that the capitalists have no reason to distribute the wealth they create. But is this true? The idea of business owners' wallowing in their ill-gotten gain is simplistic and comes mostly from literary sources; books that were written so as to sell numerous copies due to the lugubrious details contained therein.[6] No one wants to read a story about the man who does his duty, works hard, comes home to his family at night, gets up in the morning and goes about his business as before. This person may be very acceptable in God's eyes but not in a book purchaser's eyes.

Folks want to see "the human drama," even if it is a figment of the writer's imagination. People then take the details of the book, not for what they were meant—entertainment and income for the writer—but as actual, widespread conditions. This may

---

[6] The works of Charles Dickens, Sinclair Lewis, and Thomas Carlyle readily come to mind.

be why today's reader, including many Catholics, keep repeating the old canard that capitalism makes regular people poorer even though their own lives and the data do not confirm this.

This misperception results in calls for government to take steps to remedy this nonexistent situation by doing things that frustrate the very actions that will make the system work even better: additional taxes, inflationary spending, creation of an industry of "victims" by easy-to-obtain government handouts, and funding studies to "prove" that these remedies are correct, in which academics are more than willing to participate in return for government grant money.

The True Story of Wealth Creation

In discussing wealth creation one always has to remember that all social action is dependent on the actions of individuals. There is no such thing as "the system." The so-called system is the interrelationships among individuals acting as free agents. The understanding of an economy must be based on what individuals will generally do in certain situations. The first thing to note is that, as Aristotle tells us, all men act for an end or goal. The goal for which they act is based on the things that they subjectively value. We have already noted that people act to better their condition. Is this a selfish act and therefore blameworthy? I have heard people specifically misinterpret the passage in Adam Smith's *Wealth of Nations*, regarding this subject:

> But man has almost constant occasion for the help of his brethren, and it is in vain to expect it from their benevolence *only*. He will be more likely to prevail if he can interest their self-love in his favour, and shew them that it is for their own advantage to do for him what he requires of them. Whoever offers to another a bargain of this kind, proposes to do this. Give me that which I want, and you shall have this which you want, is the

> meaning of every such offer; and it is in this manner that we obtain from one another the far greater part of those good offices which we stand in need of. It is not from the benevolence of the butcher, the brewer, or the baker, that we expect our dinner, but from regard to their own interest. We address ourselves, not to their humanity but to their self-love, and never talk to them of our own necessities but of their advantages. Nobody but a beggar chuses to depend chiefly upon the benevolence of his fellow-citizens. Even a beggar does not depend on it entirely. The charity of well-disposed people, indeed, supplies him with the whole fund of his subsistence. But though this principle provides him with all necessities of life which he has occasion for, it neither does nor can provide him with them as he has occasion for them. The greater part of his occasional wants are supplied in the same manner as those of other people, by treaty, by barter, and by purchase.[7]

When Smith speaks of self-love, he is using it in the biblical sense: the basis for the force of the command to love one's neighbor as oneself.[8] God expects us to love ourselves. If we did not, we would not take care of ourselves, nor would we take steps to please God and get to heaven. Quietism was condemned as a heresy: thus, we can never say that we love God so much that we would even be satisfied to go to hell if he so desired.[9] Reginald Garrigou-Lagrange underlines this difference in his treatment of Aquinas's thought:

---

[7] Adam Smith, *An Inquiry into the Nature and Causes of the Wealth of Nations* (1976; repr., Indianapolis: Liberty Press, 1981), vol. 1, chap 2.

[8] See Lev. 19:18 and Matt 22:39, among many others.

[9] Reginald Garrigou-Lagrange, OP, *The Three Ages of the Interior Life*, vol., 2 (St. Louis: B. Herder, 1964), 291.

> St. Thomas (IIa IIae, q. 19, a. 6) clearly distinguishes between self-love which is blamable and that which is not.... "In a third way, it is indeed distinct from charity, but is not contrary thereto, as when a man loves himself from the point of view of his own good, yet not so as to place his end in this his own good": for example, if we love ourselves naturally without thereby turning away from God or disobeying his law.[10]

Therefore, seeking to better our lives is good, not to mention bettering the lives of those under our care, such as children.

What Is Capital?

If a person merely gathers food to survive, there is no way, given that there is no unexpected boon to increase his supply of gathered food, that his standard of living will increase. All his goods are used for current consumption. But, if he possesses some goods that will be used to produce consumer goods for future consumption, he possesses capital. For example, if the food gatherer invents a type of plow, he will plant some of the grain he would have consumed to begin to grow his own grain, rather than stripping the land bare and moving on. The plow is a capital good, but how did he acquire this good? He had to spend time actually thinking about his invention and how it could be made and used. To do this, he had to refrain from consuming some of his current supply of grain and save it in order to feed himself during the invention-making period when his time would be spent making and testing the plow. We call this savings. All increase in production requires savings.

Keynesians believe that capital comes from consumption—the more people consume, the greater incentive to make more of the same. This assumes a very static society. While it is true

---

[10] Garrigou-Lagrange, *The Three Ages of the Interior Life*, 368n11.

that increased sales and the subsequent rise in prices entice entrepreneurs to enter the market or to manufacture more if they are already in it, this incentive does not explain dramatic increases in the quality of goods, the complexity of goods, or the types of new goods. As an example, we will consider videotape machines. First there was the Betamax by Sony, introduced in 1975. It was a great invention because it allowed the taping of television programs. Betamax machines, however, were big, heavy, expensive, and generally meant for wealthier people with large homes. Then came the VHS machine, invented in 1976 and marketed in 1977 by the Japanese company JVC. These machines were cheaper, smaller, and easier to operate. Even though their picture quality was not as high as Betamax, they were perfectly acceptable for home use. They flew off the shelves, and the prices plunged over time, letting almost everyone have one. VHS players have since been replaced by DVD and blu-Ray technologies.

Saving implies a kind of morality. The willingness to consume less than one earns requires self-restraint. Just because we in the prosperous West are bombarded with constant pleas to purchase this or that in no way compels us to do so. Many complain about being "forced" by advertising to buy things we do not need. But all purchases are free-will actions of rational creatures. The problem is not the ads, but a materialistic mindset that, as Pope John Paul II wrote, has a person defining himself by what he has, not by what he is. Therefore, in the eyes of the materialist-consumerist, the more I have, the better I am.[11]

What are the motivations to save? First is a return on one's money. Businesses will borrow money from savers for a price—interest. The interest is the incentive for the saver to sacrifice current goods for future goods. He hopes that he will receive more goods later because of the extra money he received from

---

[11] See John Paul II, *Centesimus Annus*, no. 36.

the business than he could receive if he spent his money today. The return must exceed the rate of inflation, so as to keep the purchasing power of his money the same. If inflation is 5 percent annually, the saver needs 5 percent just to keep his purchasing power the same a year from now. If he hides his money in a mattress, it will be worth 5 percent less a year from now.

The second incentive to save is so a person will have a fund for emergencies. Illness, damage to a house that is not covered by insurance, or an unexpected funeral are examples of events that may require tapping into a supply of money that has been reserved for such emergencies. This is a reason for saving that pertains regardless of the return.

Having retirement money is another incentive to save. When a person reaches retirement, his regular income dries up. If he decided not to save for this inevitability, he will have to live on Social Security (a minimum survival level, based on solvency), or will need additional government or private assistance, or will be compelled to continue working past the customary retirement age.

In any event, regardless of the intention of the saver, savings go to expand industry, or education, or other productive endeavors. Without savings, there would be no new things: no more labor-saving devices; no better and safer cars; no central heating or running water; no central air conditioning or electric elevators; no advancements in medical diagnostics and treatments or new medicines.

Property

If you had a Ming vase in your house, and I wanted one but could not afford it, neither God's law nor the criminal code would let me take it for myself and put it on my mantelpiece. But what if I knew my sister desperately wanted a Ming vase, though neither of us could afford it, so I took yours and gave it to her? Is this not a charitable act? After all, I love my sister, and I want the best for her. I could not afford to buy this item, so I "liberated" yours. Of course, I have violated God's law and the criminal code, which prohibits theft, even if it seems to be for a good cause.

What about Robin Hood? Did he not rob from the rich and give to the poor? After all, as in the second example above, he did not directly benefit from the wealthy person's money or property; he merely liberated it to give to those who had very little. This is called the Robin Hood syndrome. The seventh commandment exists for a very good natural reason. If the goods of any of us were fair game to "do-gooders," we would find that it is hardly worth it to work. If, as soon as I came home from work with my pay or from a store with my purchases, someone could take my money or my things and give them to someone who had less, I would quickly develop a cynical attitude. I would likely decide that the more effective way to maintain or better my condition would be to steal others' things, and try to defend my stolen items as best as I could from other roving thieves.

There is another side of this problem that is important for economic development. Not only would it be chaotic and economically destructive not to secure the right to private property; not only is a person not allowed to give away a thing he has stolen, he cannot even sell it. I cannot sell what I do not own. I am not allowed to give you money entrusted to me by another. Even if I use a truck to transport air conditioners for the company for which I work, I can only use the truck for the purpose that the owner assigned to me. I am not allowed to take it off-roading or enter it in a NASCAR event. The point here is the importance of the sacredness of private property for the working of the market. Without the assurance that my property, including my money, is secure, the cynical attitude described above will develop, theft will then abound, and economic development will grind to a halt. Assuming that not everyone will obey the

Ten Commandments, there exist laws and their enforcement to assure the peaceful working of the market.

As a result, economic development and, therefore, wealth creation, requires savings, which comes from people who make more than they consume, and do so in an environment where their right to keep what they make and dispose of it is protected by law and/or custom. In addition, there needs to be a hope that they will be rewarded with a decent return when they invest the excess that they made over what they consumed. Without these factors, stagnation and widespread poverty will result.

Institutions

None of these things will occur in a society that does not have the institutions that provide the incentives for entrepreneurialism and property protection.[12] There must be enforceable rules, traditions, and customs, as well as private organizations that will encourage economic activity. If this milieu is missing, along with the entrepreneurs who can make things happen, stagnation will result.

Douglass C. North tells us that institutions affect economic performance:

> Institutions are the rules of the game in a society; more formally, they are the humanly devised constraints that shape human interaction. Thus, they structure incentives in exchange, whether political, social or economic. Institutional change shapes the way societies evolve

---

[12] For a good discussion of the role of institutions in a successful economy, see Douglass C. North, "Institutions, Ideology and Economic Performance," in *The Revolution in Development Economics*, ed. James A. Dorn, Steve H. Hanke and Alan A. Walters (Washington, DC: Cato Institute, 1998), 95–107.

through time and, hence, is the key to understanding historical change.[13]

That institutions are important to the economic well-being of a nation can be shown by looking at the Index of Economic Freedom published by the Heritage Foundation. According to this index, the number-one ranked country in 2016—that is, the country with the most economic freedom—was Hong Kong. Its per capital GDP in nominal terms (i.e., without taking inflation into account) was $42,963. The United States was ranked eleventh, and its nominal GDP was $57,294. By contrast, Uruguay was ranked forty-third, and its nominal GDP was $15,864. The general correlation between prosperity and economic freedom—which includes rule of law that protects property rights and provides equal opportunity for business creation—strongly indicates the importance of institutions. Where society's institutions do not contribute to the security of the citizen and his property, the chances for prosperous human flourishing are diminished.

Conclusion

This small book has been an attempt to show that, if Catholics are serious about improving the lives of the poor, we must be serious about understanding the sources of wealth creation. The intention and the will to help the poor are indispensable, and the social teaching of the Church has done much to stimulate Catholics and others to action on behalf of the marginalized. I submit that more reflection on and analysis of the historical causes of wealth and poverty, with an emphasis on the findings of the discipline of economics, would make the Church's specific recommendations for action and policies more convincing

---

[13] North, "Institutions, Ideology, and Economic Performance," 95.

and effective. The present work is but a small start. There are many obstacles to wealth creation that lay beyond the scope of this discussion, among them political strife; the confiscation of wealth by tyrants; forced industrialization of agrarian societies; overregulation by government; and high taxation. Solving these problems is no easy task, but the monumental job of curing poverty cannot succeed if it does not begin with an accurate understanding of how to create wealth.

References

Church Documents and Early Christian Sources

Tertullian, *Apology*.

St. John Chrysostom, *On Wealth and Poverty*. Translated by Catharine P. Roth. Crestwood, NY: St. Vladimir's Seminary Press, 1984.

St. Augustine, *The City of God*.

St. Thomas Aquinas, *Summa Theologica*.

Pope Leo XIII, Encyclical Letter *Rerum Novarum* (1891).

Pope Pius XI, Encyclical Letter *Quadragesimo Anno* (1931).

Pope Paul VI, Encyclical Letter *Populorum Progressio* (1967).

Pope John Paul II, Encyclical Letter *Laborem Exercens* (1981).

Pope John Paul II, "Biblical Account of Creation Analyzed." In *Original Unity of Man and Woman: Catechesis on the Book of Genesis* (Boston: St. Paul Editions, 1981).

Pope John Paul II, Encyclical Letter *Centesimus Annus* (1991).

Pope Benedict XVI, Encyclical Letter *Caritas in Veritate* (2009).

Secondary Sources

Barclay, William. *The Gospel of Luke*, rev. ed. Philadelphia: Westminster Press, 1975.

Bauer, Peter. "The Disregard of Reality." In *The Revolution in Development Economics*. Washington, DC: Cato Institute, 1998.

Beck, Joseph Charles et al. "Care of the Poor by the Church." *The Catholic Encyclopedia*. New York: Robert Appleton, 1911. Available at http://www.newadvent.org/cathen/12236a.htm.

Becker, Gary S. *The Economics of Discrimination*. Chicago: University of Chicago Press, 1971.

Bedouelle, Guy, OP. *St. Dominic: The Grace of the Word*. San Francisco: Ignatius Press, 1987.

Booth, Philip. *International Aid and Integral Human Development*. Grand Rapids: Acton Institute, 2011.

Buchanan, James. *The Collected Works of James M. Buchanan*. Vol. 7. *The Limits of Liberty: Between Anarchy and Leviathan*. Indianapolis: Liberty Fund, 2000.

Costanzo, Joseph, SJ. *Political and Legal Studies*. Vol. 1. *Politeia*. West Hanover, MA: Christopher Publishing, 1982.

Daniel-Rops, Henri. *Daily Life in the Time of Jesus*. Translated by Patrick O'Brian. New York: Hawthorn Books, 1962.

Dean, Herbert A. *The Social and Political Ideas of St. Augustine*. New York: Columbia University Press, 1963.

De Soto, Hernando. *The Mystery of Capital: Why Capitalism Triumphs in the West and Fails Everywhere Else*. New York: Basic Books, 2000.

De Soto, Jesús Huerta. *Money, Bank Credit and Economic Cycles*. Auburn, AL: Ludwig von Mises Institute, 2006.

Garrigou-Lagrange, Reginald, OP. *The Three Ages of the Interior Life*. 2 vols. St. Louis: B. Herder, 1964.

Giordani, Igino. *The Social Message of Jesus*. Boston: St. Paul Editions, 1977.

Giordani, Igino. *The Social Message of the Church Fathers*. Boston: St. Paul Editions, 1977.

Hackelman, Jac C., ed. *Readings in Public Choice Economics*. Ann Arbor: University of Michigan Press, 2004.

Higgs, Robert. "Public Choice and Political Leadership." In *Against Leviathan: Government Power and the Free Society*. Oakland, CA: Independent Institute, 2004.

Jacobs, Jane. *The Economy of Cities*. New York: Vintage, 1970.

Jouvenel, Bertrand de. *Sovereignty: An Inquiry into the Political Good*. 1957. Reprint, Indianapolis: Liberty Fund, 1997.

Kennedy, Robert G. "Does a Business Corporation Have a Responsibility to Society?" *Religion and Liberty* 13 (November/December 2003).

Ketteler, Wilhelm Emmanuel von. *The Social Teachings of Wilhelm Emmanuel von Ketteler: Bishop of Mainz (1811–1877)*. Edited by Rupert J. Ederer. Washington, DC: University Press of America, 1981.

Luckey, William R. "Suggestions on Rebuilding Catholic Social Teachings on Economics." *Journal of the Institute of Economic Affairs* 30, no. 1 (2010).

Luckey, William R. "The Intellectual Origins of Modern Catholic Social Teachings on Economics." Available at https://www.scribd.com/document/105782660/William-Luckey.

Marx, Karl. *The Manifesto of the Communist Party*. In *The Marx-Engels Reader*. Edited by Robert C. Tucker. Second revised and enlarged edition. New York: W. W. Norton, 1978.

McGregor, Douglas. *The Human Side of Enterprise*. New York: McGraw-Hill, 1960.

References

Menger, Carl. *Principles of Economics*. 1871. Reprint, New York: New York University Press, 1981.

Mill, John Stuart. *Principles of Political Economy*. 1848. Reprint, London: Longmans, Green and Co. 1909. Publishing information available at http://www.econlib.org/library/Mill/mlP.html.

Mises, Ludwig von. "The Origin of Money," in *The Theory of Money and Credit* (New Haven, CT: Yale University Press, 1953)

North, Douglass C. "Institutions, Ideology and Economic Performance." In *The Revolution in Development Economics*. Edited by James A. Dorn, Steve H. Hanke, and Alan A. Walters. Washington, DC: Cato Institute, 1998.

Rider, Christine. *Introduction to Economic History*. Cincinnati: South-Western College Publishing, 1995.

Rothbard, Murray. *Man, Economy and the State with Power and Market*. Auburn, AL: Ludwig von Mises Institute, 2004.

Simon, Julian L. *The State of Humanity*. Oxford: Blackwell, 1995.

Smith, Adam. *An Inquiry into the Nature and Causes of the Wealth of Nations*. 1776. Reprint, Indianapolis: Liberty Classics, 1981.

Tullock, Gordon. *The Selected Works of Gordon Tullock*. Vol. 1. *Virginia Political Economy*. Indianapolis: Liberty Fund, 2004.

Vinogradoff, Sir Paul, "Feudalism." In *The Cambridge Medieval History*. Cambridge: Cambridge University Press, 1968.

Voegelin, Eric. *The New Science of Politics*. Chicago: University of Chicago Press, 1952.

Woods, Thomas E., Jr. "The Unanswered Questions of the Just Wage." In *Catholic Social Teaching and the Market Economy*. Edited by Philip Booth. London: Institute of Economic Affairs, 2007.

About the Author

Dr. William R. Luckey is professor emeritus of political science and economics at Christendom College where he has taught since 1984. Born in the south Bronx, New York City, he received his BA from St. John's University, New York, and served in the United States Marine Corps. He received an MA and a PhD in political philosophy from Fordham University where he was a student of Father Francis P. Canavan, SJ, and was an Earhart Foundation Fellow and a Robert Boone Stewart Fellow. He taught at St. John's University, St. Francis College in Brooklyn, and Cardinal Newman College in St. Louis prior to coming to Christendom. He holds an MBA from Shenandoah University and an MA in economics from George Mason University where he was a student of Nobel Prize-winner James Buchanan. In addition, he has an MA in systematic theology and a certificate in dogmatic theology from the Notre Dame Graduate School of Christendom College

He has published in *Faith and Reason*, the *Journal of Markets and Morality*, and the *Homiletic and Pastoral Review*. He is the author of "John Courtney Murray: A Catholic Appreciation" in *John Courtney Murray and the American Civil Conversation*, edited by Kenneth Grasso and Robert Hunt and has given scholarly papers at Franciscan University of Steubenville, Calvin College, Auburn University, the Eric Voegelin Society, and the

About the Author

American Political Science Association. Luckey is an adjunct scholar of the Ludwig von Mises Institute and is on the Board of Scholars of the Virginia Institute for Public Policy Studies.

He has been married for forty-six years and has four children and twenty-two grandchildren. He has been a member of the Third Order of St. Dominic for over forty years.